OAKLAND
ATHLETICS
STARS, STATS, HISTORY, AND MORE!
BY CONOR BUCKLEY

Published by The Child's World®
1980 Lookout Drive • Mankato, MN 56003-1705
800-599-READ • www.childsworld.com

ISBN 9781503828339
LCCN 2018944847

Printed in the United States of America
PAO2392

Photo Credits:
Cover: Joe Nicholson/USA Today Sports;
AP Photos (inset).
Interior: Alamy Stock Photo: Zuma Press 20, 29;
AP Images: 6, Matt York 10, 17, Rusty Kennedy 19, 23;
Dreamstime.com: Lawrence Wesolowski Jr. 14;
Library of Congress: 9; Newscom: Andrew Dieb/Icon SMI
27; Joe Robbins 5, 24; Shutterstock: Trekandshoot 13.

About the Author

Conor Buckley is a lifelong baseball fan now studying for a career in esports. His books in this series are his first published works.

On the Cover

Main photo: Khris "Khrush" Davis
Inset: Hall of Famer Reggie Jackson

CONTENTS

GO, ATHLETICS!

The Oakland Athletics have been playing in the Major Leagues since 1901. The team is usually called the A's. The ball club has won nine **World Series**. That's the third most in MLB history! Although they haven't won the title since 1989, the A's have reached the playoffs 10 times since then. Let's meet this championship team!

A's ace Daniel Mengden has a great fastball and a cool mustache! ➤

WHO ARE THE ATHLETICS?

The Oakland Athletics play in the American League (AL). That group is part of Major League Baseball (MLB). MLB also includes the National League (NL). There are 30 teams in MLB. The winner of the NL plays the winner of the AL in the World Series. Three of the A's nine World Series wins came in a row—1972, 1973, and 1974!

◄ *The A's dogpile after winning the 1974 World Series. It was their third in a row!*

WHERE THEY CAME FROM

The Athletics were formed in 1901. They were one of the original eight teams to play in the American League. They played in Philadelphia until 1955. That year, they moved to Kansas City. They didn't stay there long. The team moved to Oakland, California, in 1968 and has played there ever since.

This baseball card from 1910 shows Connie Mack, ➤
who was the Philadelphia A's manager for 50 years.

WORLD'S CHAMPIONS

1910.

MACK, Mgr., ATHLETICS

WHO THEY PLAY

The Athletics play 162 games in a season. That's a lot of baseball! They play most of their games against other AL teams. The Athletics are part of the AL West Division. The other AL West teams are the Houston Astros, the Los Angeles Angels, the Seattle Mariners, and the Texas Rangers. The A's also play NL teams. The Athletics have a big **rival** in the NL's San Francisco Giants, who play nearby.

◄ *Khris Davis scores as the A's battle their rivals, the Giants.*

WHERE THEY PLAY

The Athletics play their home games at the Oakland Coliseum. They share the stadium with the Oakland Raiders of the National Football League (NFL). They are the only team in the MLB to share their stadium with an NFL team. The A's also used to share the stadium with the San Jose Earthquakes soccer team. The A's are hoping to move into a new ballpark someday.

The Oakland Coliseum is big enough for ➤
football and soccer teams to play there, too.

THE BASEBALL FIELD

FOUL LINE ◀

SECOND BASE ▼

THIRD BASE ▼

PITCHER'S MOUND ▲

COACH'S BOX ◀

HOME PLATE ▶

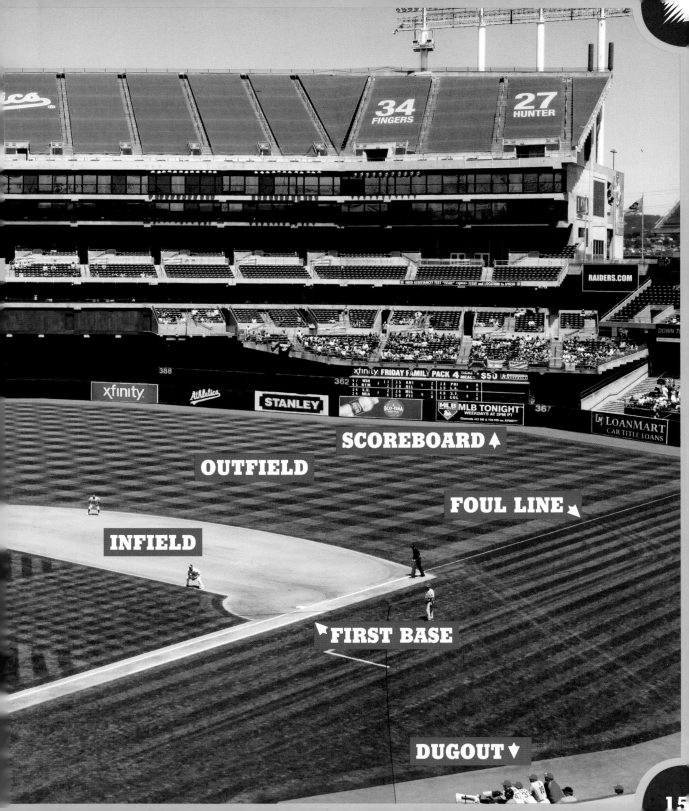

34 FINGERS

27 HUNTER

RAIDERS.COM

388

xfinity **FRIDAY FAMILY PACK** 4 TICKETS MEALS $50

xfinity

Athletics

STANLEY

ECO-FINA BOTTLE

MLB **MLB TONIGHT**
WEEKDAYS AT 3PM PT

362

367

LoanMart
CAR TITLE LOANS

SCOREBOARD ▲

OUTFIELD

FOUL LINE ▶

INFIELD

◀ FIRST BASE ▶

DUGOUT ▼

BIG DAYS

The Athletics are one of the oldest teams in the AL. They have been winning ever since they were founded. Here are some of their best performances.

1929—These Athletics had one of the best **lineups** ever. The team featured four future Hall of Famers, including pitcher Lefty Grove and first baseman Al Simmons. The A's won 104 games, the most in the AL. They faced the Chicago Cubs in the World Series. Philadelphia won in five games. In one of those games, they came from eight runs behind to win!

While with the A's, Lefty Grove led the AL in strikeouts seven times! ➤

1972–74—In 1972, the A's were champs in their fifth season in Oakland. They were led by future Hall of Famers Reggie Jackson, Catfish Hunter, and Rollie Fingers. In all, they won three World Series in a row.

2002—The A's had lost three of their top players. They didn't have much money to sign new ones. **General manager** Billy Beane thought of new ways to find top players. His ideas worked. The A's did well! Beane's plan was later in a book called *Moneyball*.

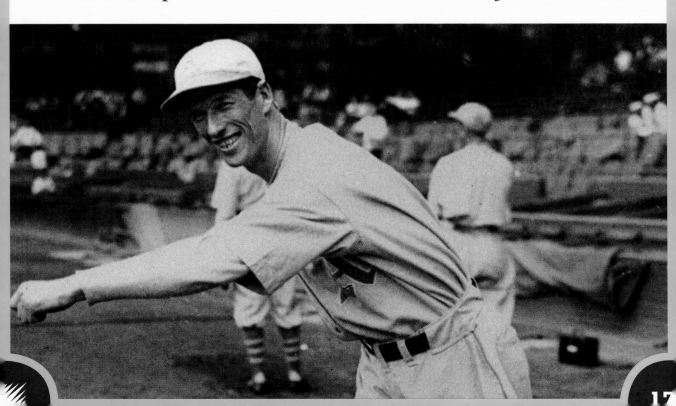

TOUGH DAYS

Every season can't end with a title. Here's a look back at some games and seasons Athletics fans might want to forget!

1915–1921—The A's finished last in the AL seven years in a row!

1988—The A's were upset in the World Series by the Los Angeles Dodgers. L.A.'s injured star hitter, Kirk Gibson, hit a **walkoff** home run in Game 1. The A's went on to lose the Series 4–1.

2014—The A's made it to the **Wild Card** Playoff Game. Then they lost to the Kansas City Royals.

Kirk Gibson's homer to beat the A's in 1988 ➤
is one of the most famous in baseball history.

MEET THE FANS!

The Athletics may have one of baseball's oddest **mascots**. An elephant has cheered on the team since 1902. Back then, a rival manager insulted the A's, calling them a "white elephant." (That is slang for "something useless.") Manager Connie Mack didn't care. He made that the team's mascot. Even today, A's players wear a white elephant on their uniforms. In Oakland, an elephant mascot named Stomper entertains fans!

◄ *Stomper can be found roaming the stands at the Oakland Coliseum.*

HEROES THEN

The Athletics have had 15 Hall of Famers! Connie Mack led the A's for 50 years as the team's manager. That's the most in baseball history. **Slugger** Jimmie Foxx was one of Mack's stars. The big first baseman hit 534 home runs. In the 1970s, outfielder Reggie Jackson helped the A's win three World Series. Jose Canseco and Mark McGwire were together known as the "Bash Brothers." They combined for 446 home runs in the seven years they were on the A's together.

The great Babe Ruth posed with fellow slugger Jimmie Foxx. ➤

Oakland's current team is filled with young stars. The best is Khris "Khrush" Davis. The outfielder has the most home runs of any hitter in MLB since 2016. In 2018, shortstop Jed Lowrie was among the AL leaders in runs batted in (RBI). Blake Treinen is a hard-throwing relief pitcher. Off the field, Billy Beane is the brains behind the A's. He uses new stats and math to find great new A's players.

◄ *In 2018, Jed Lowrie had his best season as a hitter.*

GEARING UP

Baseball players wear team uniforms. On defense, they wear leather gloves to catch the ball. As batters, they wear hard helmets. This protects them from pitches. Batters hit the ball with long wood bats. Each player chooses his own size of bat. Catchers have the toughest job. They wear a lot of protection.

THE BASEBALL

The outside of the Major League baseball is made from cow leather. Two leather pieces shaped like 8s are stitched together. There are 108 stitches of red thread. These stitches help players grip the ball. Inside, the ball has a small center of cork and rubber. Hundreds of feet of yarn are tightly wound around this center.

← CATCHER'S MASK AND HELMET

CHEST PROTECTOR →

◄ CATCHER'S MITT

SHIN GUARDS →

CATCHER'S GEAR

TEAM STATS

ere are some of the all-time career records for the Oakland Athletics. All these stats are through the 2018 regular season.

HOME RUNS	
Mark McGwire	363
Jimmie Foxx	302

RBI	
Al Simmons	1,179
Jimmie Foxx	1.075

BATTING AVERAGE	
Al Simmons	.356
Jimmie Foxx	.339

STRIKEOUTS	
Eddie Plank	1,985
Rube Waddell	1,576

WINS	
Eddie Plank	284
Lefty Grove	195

SAVES	
Dennis Eckersley	320
Rollie Fingers	136

Rickey Henderson was with the A's in 1990 when he ➤ became baseball's all-time stolen base leader.

STOLEN BASES	
Rickey Henderson	867
Bert Campaneris	566

GLOSSARY

general manager (JENN-er-ul MAN-uh-jur) the person who runs a baseball team off the field, choosing players to add and hiring the field manager

lineups (LYN-upz) the lists of players appearing in a game

mascots (MASS-cots) costumed characters who help fans cheer

rivals (RYE-vuhls) two people or groups competing for the same thing

slugger (SLUG-er) a player who hits a lot of homers or extra-base hits

walkoff (WAWK-off) a hit that ends a game for the home team

Wild Card (WYLD KARD) a playoff team that did not win its division

World Series (WURLD SEE-reez) the annual championship of Major League Baseball between winners of the AL and NL

FIND OUT MORE

IN THE LIBRARY

Connery-Boyd, Peg. *The MLB Big Book of Baseball Activities*. Chicago, IL: Sourcebooks Jabberwocky, 2016.

Sports Illustrated for Kids (editors). *The Big Book of Who: Baseball*. New York, NY: Liberty Street, 2017.

Stewart, Mark. *The Oakland Athletics* (Team Spirit). Chicago, IL: Norwood House, 2012.

ON THE WEB

Visit our website for links about the Oakland Athletics:
childsworld.com/links

Note to Parents, Teachers, and Librarians: We routinely verify our web links to make sure they are safe and active sites. So encourage your readers to check them out!

INDEX